Ifor Thomas was born in Haverfordw[...]

> "My son pokes fun at my disi[...]
> I arrive back on the beach af[...]
> exhausted. Later he says my b[...]
> I don't remember talking to my father that way.
> Sun has stopped the acne which is chipping
> the fresh marble of his cheeks like shrapnel
> but it will be back, I know.
> I've been there, and
> given everything
> here is not so bad." (Here)

He was one of the founders of Cabaret 246 and The Horse's Mouth. He has been performing his work since the early 'eighties.

> "He is the most ferocious performance poet I've ever seen."
> (Duncan Bush)

He writes about clingfilm; the ageing process; sex...

> "His poems are tales ... things that happen to South Wales
> marrieds, with kids, with houses," (Peter Finch)

.... and Julie Walters.

> "Ifor Thomas has a terrible talent," (Julie Walters)

He has performed at festivals including the Cardiff, Newport and Swansea Festivals of Literature, and four times at the Hay Literature Festival. He won the John Tripp Award for Spoken Poetry in 1992 and the Welsh writer's prize in 1995 Cardiff International Poetry Competition. His further literary endeavours include radio and television performances; reviews and articles in publications including *Planet* and *The New Welsh Review*; his poetry has been published in *Poetry Wales, Yellow Crane, SWAGMAG*, and more. He moonlights as an architect, and lives in Cardiff.

PARTHIAN BOOKS

Unsafe Sex

Ifor Thomas

PARTHIAN BOOKS

Parthian Books
53 Colum Road
Cardiff
CF10 3EF

First published in 1999.
All rights reserved.
© Ifor Thomas
ISBN 1 902638 05 0

Typeset in Galliard by NW.

Printed and bound by ColourBooks, Dublin 13,
Ireland.

The publishers would like to thank the Arts Council of
Wales for support in the publication of this book.

With support from the Parthian Collective.

Cover: 'Starting Out' oil on linen 1998 85 x 110cm by
Kevin Sinnott,
Martin Tinney Gallery

A CIP catalogue record for this book is available from
the British Library.

For Gill, Mollie & Dan,

How did they put up with it ?

Publications:

poetry:

> Giving Blood (1985)
> Giving Blood 2 (1987)
> Bogwiser (1991)
> Pubic (1995)

fiction:

> The Stuff of Love (1993)

> All published by Red Sharks Press

UNSAFE SEX

PUBIC (1995)

BOGWISER (1991)

GIVING BLOOD 2 (1987)

When your wife suspects you of having an affair

She will wait until you have entered the kitchen
before sniffing the air, and touching your shoulder
as if you were stuffed with horsehair.

She will stare into your eyes, for the image of a lover
will be imprinted there, then ask:
What was the weather at three this afternoon?

She will inspect your car with a magnifying glass
dust the dash for fingerprints, look for lint,
dirt or sand. There will be questions to answer.

She will check mileage, tyre pressures;
the angle of inclination of the seat,
then raise the bonnet, drain oil.

She will take your mobile phone
break it under the heel of her boot,
sift the fragments for strange numbers.

She will open a vein to take blood samples,
analyse your stomach contents
to check for fish, rich food and mangoes.

She will cut through your scrotum while you sleep,
dissect your vas to uncover recent sperm movements,
explore further, touch the prostate - find it stiffening.

She will lie next to you,
wait for your lips to mutter another's name,
watch your eyelids flicker in your nightmare.

She will cleave your skull with an axe,
dip her fingers into the images that fall out of
your optic nerve, is the brain still hot?

Then at the weekend you will have a smoke,
share a bottle of wine and she will laugh
as you tell her somebody else's joke.

Fragments of You

Ice has turned the white of a blind dog's eyes -
like that collie at the end of our street, despised
by all the children except you, reaching out
over the gate to rub its snout on the way to school,
me rushing on, pretending you weren't my sister.

I received your card today.
Your handwriting is barely legible
words find their way by memory,
stumble up one side, fall over the other.
Your daughter has checked it, put in corrections -
her writing looks like yours did as a girl.

I visit the sculpture a short walk along the bay,
this shining sphere looks as if it's fallen from
a giant's bagatelle board. That game we used to play-
neat nail heads in lines, rings, clusters
round which the ball randomly clattered.
Over the sea's edge dunlin weave in flight,
white wings playing tag with the light
as if sun's rays had been frozen, shattered,
tossed to swirl in the brittle air.

The sculpture has been vandalised,
the spyhole glass broken, thick and green like ice
from the ornamental pool scattered
over gravel by Harry Ramsden's takeaway.
Bent by mirrors through the sphere, slipped and distorted
soon to be lost forever, the views of the bay.

You were braver than your brother at accepting a dare.
Once we raced along the side of Albany chapel
hands dragging on the render. I cheated there.
But you shamed me with the proof of bleeding fingers.
That time too when we went to see King Lear,

you held my hand as Laughton had his eyes put out -
did you have a premonition,
or was it your way of dealing with fear?

You write - *a failure of the optic nerve*
all I can see is fragments
(Julia writes *of you* in the margin with a query)
I'm weary of tests - there comes a point
when you just have to make do.

I turn away from the sculpture,
the wind winds in from the west
Pushing the fading light before it,
cold enough to tear tears from my eyes.

Steam

You cut off our conversation by flouncing off into the shower
a last glimpse of your breasts as they bobbed away
then the angry hiss of hot water against the glass door.
I wait downstairs, you don't say goodbye.
Your car turns out of the street, and I guess
you don't even check the rear view.
I wander the house, hospitable as an abattoir
memories bump me like hanging carcasses.
Then I open the shower door, release your steam.

The loved one

The cadaver is white as suet,
split like a carcass of beef, organs removed.

In the adjoining room the pathologist
drains lungs, applies callipers to the spinal stem.
He's cleaved bone, cracked ribs,
made notes in a spiral pad, eaten a sandwich.

The assistant wonders how he'll put this lot together.
After he's hosed the floor, she'll come to view.

She will ask to touch the loved one's hand,
kiss his perfect pallor. She will be refused,
sit the other side of a screen, feel her breath cloud,
remember his last slow dance around the kitchen table.

Valentine's Day poetry reading

It's a bad venue and only a dozen people.
Tonight we are celebrating love,
and isn't poetry the only way to do it?

The first reader canters through the usual stuff
but we are really here for the medieval erotic verse,
and it doesn't disappoint.

The professor goes at it
crunching up the Welsh language
biting off big gobs full.

The bards of the middle ages
didn't mess around
they went at each other hammer and tongs.

There's silence - we savour his performance.
These poems still crackle after five hundred years.
Then there is the scraping of a chair.

A question perhaps?
She stands still, then speaks:
How dare you read such poems?

Heads turn as she delivers her attack
Serial adulterer…abuser of women… and me.
She faces him down, leaves.

Woman on man, man on woman.
It takes the lens of thwarted love
to see a real arsehole.

Eating Rainbows

Graham has caved in.
The flesh has gone from his face,
he walks as if gravity
has developed a force field especially for him.

He visited an alternative therapist
who recommended he eat only rainbows
and even then not the colour purple
as that has been made into a film by Spielberg
and celluloid is bad for the colon
(It also collects around the buttocks).

Siân is dressed in white:
her face shines - she looks like a candle.
She whispers to me:
Graham is the fuel of my life.

He smiles,
loving her to death.

House Party

The first neighbour arrives to complain
after the band has been playing
for ten minutes. Others come at regular intervals
saying the baby/husband/wife/dog has been woken
and when will there be quiet?

The police officer arrives during the second set.
I apologise for keeping her waiting at the door
the band was too noisy to hear the bell.
She enters the premises to check for drugs
and bad people.

Terry the boxer arrives and dances with the police officer
her handcuffs jangle, people call out *Hi Louise.*
As I show her to the door she says:
Aren't some people miserable - you carry on,.
if they argue say PC Paine said so.

The lone vigilante arrives at four a.m.
I answer the door to a man who says
I'm calling to pay you back for keeping me awake with your
noise.
Then he disappears into the dawn; and I haven't even gone
to bed yet.

Feel Fat

I come home from the weekend conference
feel Fat
it was about food
with a tiny bit on famine

I weigh myself
I'm heavier than ever before
11stone 13lbs

I shit
weigh myself again
11stone 11lbs

I take off all my clothes
11stone 6lbs

I cut my finger
toe nails
pluck hair from nose
clean wax from my ears
comb dandruff from my head
have a shower and scrub my skin with a Brillo pad
masturbate
sneeze
sweat
spit
11stone 5.99lbs

I confess to my wife past sins and misdemeanours
she says
I bet that's a weight off your mind
I nod
return to the weighing scales.

Sex Manual

It's risky to spy on your lover in the nude
hide your eyes with your fingers
or wear welding goggles.

Ask her on a train journey
but don't make love.
The fat man is watching.

Invite her to eat
it's easier to lie
on a full stomach.

Beware of crushing garlic with a knife
between her legs because
one slip and there's no point.

When you remove the layers of her clothing
pretend she is an onion
let tears fill your eyes.

Make love gently.
Recite pin numbers.
Remember you are unlocking her heart.

Don't hold your breath at the moment of orgasm
or you will discover eternity -
the last thing you want.

Instead breathe slowly,
even when your heart beats 200 to the minute.
Medicine has made enormous advances.

There is a decompression chamber in Birmingham
for those who come to the surface too quickly
or have watched too many videos.

And when it's over
don't rush to leave.
Knowing your luck, it's raining hard.

Bomber

After fifty-six years the aluminium is slate grey
and the ribs of the wings as light as bird bones.
Wind rattles through the remains of the bomber
that failed to clear the escarpment of Cwar y Cigfan.

The walkers rest here, throw a ball for the dog,
drink beer, share a bag of crisps, lean against the rough
memorial.
The wreaths of last November have moulted their poppies,
there is a wooden cross jammed between stones.

It's a long way home for the five Canadians
whose names are now barely legible.
Above, a hang glider hovers on the edge of a thermal
then skitters into a mocking dive.

Clouds are solid enough to reach up and grab
like the craggy hand that pulled these airmen to earth
splattered their blood over the stones and sheep shit of Cwar
y Cigfan
made them forever part of Wales.

The genius - *Yea*

In the doctor's waiting room
the magazines are old - Autocar 1997,
Good Housekeeping, last autumn.
There's even a Rubic cube -
when did you last see one of those?
The boy's dressed in Jordan Chicago Bulls,
Wales Umbro, Adidas and Nike Air.
He picks up the cube, starts unpeeling
the coloured squares, face frozen in concentration.
His girlfriend returns with a prescription.
He says look - I've solved the cube
She turns it in her hand -
Each facet is now one colour.
Wow, you're a genius.
Yea.

If the door squeaks

Only four people know the formula for WD40,
they must travel separately and never be in the same room.
Each keeps a can in a locked safe.

Only four people know the formula for Coca-Cola,
They too must take precautions against tragedy
and keep a can in a locked safe.

One person knows that the formula for WD40
is the same as Coca-Cola except
for the addition of nitrogen gas and colouring.

He keeps two cans in his safe, must not be seen putting
Coca-Cola
on squeaky door hinges. Although once, at a dinner party,
he did squirt WD40 into a guest's glass of rum.

Being Anthony Perkins

You look like Anthony Perkins,
says a man who turns out to be
the architectural critic of *The Times.*

We're at Paul's memorial service -
in the Imagination gallery.
Women in black stretch mine,
men in white serve canapés,
food like the innards of a watch.

After my reading of the poem
the critic's demeanour changes
but he won't tell me how old he is.

It's either the cheese,
or he smells like a goat.

He says:
I'm writing a biography of Frink,
Moya is up there with Le Corb and Frank.
The inspiration for the Woolsenhome building
was a pomegranate and black grapes.

A waiter trips with his tray.
The crash of glass is clean and sharp
wine spatters the pure white drapes.
In my mind a shower curtain shivers.

Musicians on the bridge continue to play.

His wife, eyes cutting me to shreds,
leads the critic away.

Australian Sketches

Party night
Glenno, shades, pony tail
gut, beard, speech slowed
by smoking at least a couple of cones
cold stubby in his fist

You a Pom?
No, Welsh.

Welsh, Irish, Scottish, Cornish, Geordie, Cockney
Scouser, Brummie, Belfuckingfast - you're all poms

Yes, I'm a pom.

Tiger
Mark's been so long in the Outback
he looks like an aborigine,
except he wears a leather hat.
In his garden he stands on one leg
flicks a spent match at the Tiger snake
coiled in a tree trunk.
It sways its head
confused by the smell
of smoke and sulphur,
flicks its tongue between fangs
loaded with enough venom to kill
a million mice with one bite.
Mark draws on his cigarette
shifts onto his other leg.

> *If bitten wrap the wound tightly*
> *Do not apply a tourniquet, do not cut, do not suck.*
> *If bitten on the head or neck, don't bother.*

He calls, Tiger! Tiger!
like me to the cat at home.

One of us

Dead, his reputation is being rewritten
in the speeches, drunken asides,
in the conversations of old women
with their heart throb, the undertaker.

Heat from his ashes warms the worms
as the cannon's cape, with its cat's clasp,
drips rain in the vestry. Its owner
takes tea with a dash of whisky.

His children, with their children already
beyond understanding, now wonder
if they ever knew their father
as together and individually

they try to make sense of a life
that was different for all of them.
Yet on this point they agree:
he was one of us.

Taking Tea

I agree to tea. She opens a packet,
unfolding the foil so that each leaf
falls into the caddy. She heaps teaspoons,
black as mouse droppings, into the china pot.

As she pours water, her face clouds.
She passes me the mug with elaborate care,
as if its liquid is too dangerous.
I sit like a boxer, breathing towely tea fumes.

There is little to say, not even the past is
worth arguing over. Two-handed,
I drain the mug. She asks if I want
my fortune read in tea leaves. I decline.

She did that once, ten years ago,
And every word came true.

The Opening

It was the minister's job
to open the new facility.
A dour Presbyterian,
not known for his humour,
he cut the ribbon and declared
that the entrance arch
would be enhanced
by a clitoris.
I think he means clematis,
whispered the mayor.
And, continued the minister
some ivy over the top
could represent the pubic hair.

Wheat-Free-Pete's Prayer

Not even rolls which art unleaven
gluten free be the game.
Thy rice cakes come
no more toast will be done,
nor pasta even if it taste like heaven
give us this day our daily quorn
and forgive us wanting Yorkshire pudding
as we forgive them their lumpy gravy
and lead us not to the pub to drink beer
for wine is the thing and will be less gory
not IPA nor SA again.
Amen.

Piano Protest

A man walked into Steinway's
and locked himself inside
the best upright piano in the showroom.
By means of messages written
on the sheet music of Russ Conway
he let it be known that
he was conducting a protest
at the trend of replacing
real music with digital sound.
He said his name was Joanna.
Steinways were frightened -
there was a spate of
copy cat piano protests
by a group of Liberace lookalikes.
After a week he emerged.
The deal was he got a slot
on Red Dragon Radio
and the opportunity
to push one sampler organ
over a cliff of his choice.

The Harbour Master's Funeral

They slow, cresting the hill,
the engine labours, hearse shudders.
Behind, cars of the cortege
are strung out on the coast road.

His sailor's peaked cap moves
on the flag covered coffin.
Turning to take one last look at the sea.
I can almost hear his voice.

Later his plastic urn
will be placed in the ground
this hole, a foot by a foot,
the neatest he's been for a long time.

His life sprawled through ours,
in the same way that
his spaniel shook the sea
over sunbathers on the quay.

Even to that great fight
when he threatened to piss
against the public toilet wall
if the council insisted he pay.

And they relented,
as did his wife over him boiling
crabs and lobsters in the best saucepan,
fixing the boat engine on the lawn.

To him tourists were fair game
lucky to get a decent mooring
but he always had enough time
to show a kid how to tie a fishing line.

His children finished his collection
of miniature malts as he lay dying,
only the drop of Glenfiddich
caused his lips to twitch,

the smile of a ghost.
The rest of this winter will see
Sharkey's office empty,
until spring tides run to the sand quay.

I have a hangover and the vet is an Elvis fan

His fingers force open the cat's jaws.
In the Elvis look-a-like competition he came third.
Mr Presley underwent his terminal event
when he was on the commode
his insides had compacted with a clay-like substance
putting so much pressure on his cholesterol-furred heart that
his aorta burst.
The vet shows me enlarged photos of fleas
then gives the cat a shot of steroids
and me a tube of powder to dust my carpet.
At the reception desk I write a cheque
as the vet shapes an imaginary quiff in the mirror.

Weather Forecast

Patterson has settled himself into my office.
His voice is like the weather forecast.
It drones on and by the time he's finished
I don't know whether it's going to rain in Wales
because I stopped listening around the Midlands.
The wind rattles a blind:
Do you agree that's the best way forward?
Yes, yes, of course I say.
He shuts the window and I open
an umbrella in my mind.

Christmas Drink

In Kilner jars, sloe gin
stood in our kitchen.
Pierced berries clumped
like path lab specimens,
trapped ectoplasm
or diseased organs.
Clear liquid turned pink,
then days later the black
of coagulated blood.

He and I sat through
that Christmas holiday,
occasionally sipping sloe gin,
with little to say.

I watched the colour of the fluid in
my father's collostomy bag
change from black to urine,
as his rebored urethra healed
so that he could begin
to piss again.

Post Christmas Drink

How was Christmas for you?
I ask the barman
waiting for a Guinness to settle.

Christ I nearly died
woke up Christmas eve could hardly breathe
rushed into hospital left lung collapsed
never happened before, no warning
gave me drugs, had to pump it up
spent three days in intensive care
now here I am second day of the New Year
working like a dog.

He applies the finishing touches,
traces a lucky four leaf clover in the froth.
Have one for yourself I say.

The Future

This is the book of my childhood -
Every Boy's Annual 1932
(The Most Up To Date Boys' Annual In The World).
Bought in a chapel jumble sale
sometime in the Fifties.
The cover photograph biplane vanishes into a snowstorm
of peeling colour, scratched sea receding
from the rounded brown cardboard corners.

It predicted a future of airships
steam trains, cars with long bonnets,
and even then my radio was nothing like this wireless
of crystals and an aerial that swung
from a post into the house.
Schoolboys, with buttoned blazers, caps,
and pulled up socks, demonstrated how
to solder old tins
make a leather sucker
a hydroplane for half-a-crown
a jumping frog.
I learnt by heart
the components of an airship mooring mast.

I showed it to my son: *there's no colour, no computers
no guns, no war,* he said with the
tired wisdom of a Nineties teenager.
And who cares about fretwork?

I closed the cover on its broken spine -
1932, when the Nazis became the largest party
in the Reichstag, and Europe toppled into chaos.
A good time, for sure, to learn how to make a jumping frog.

Reading

The party was an end of term affair.
She held the cracked coffee cup in her hand
which I had just picked at random
from the clutter of the worktop.
She tipped its contents on the oil cloth
between the pools of beer.

One fish earring
free pint of Guinness coin
dry green rubber
button badge, red enamelled
two kroner coin
two 10 groschen coins
hair clip
one fish earring
13 amp fuse
drawing pin
safety pins
collar stud inscribed "eternal"
crystal of broken glass
dried leaf
nails.

She sifted the objects like tarot cards,
told me the signs were strong.

The glass was a glimpse of things to come;
the fish meant travel,
the fuse; impatience with fools,
the Guinness coin was a welcome release,
the foreign coins an obsession with the trivial,
the red badge indicated courage obviously,
safety pins money, albeit pin money;
drawing pin, creativity.

Of the collar stud she would not elaborate:
the nails made her sad.
The leaf she crumpled between her fingers;
the hair clip she slipped into her pocket.
I noticed she had not mentioned the dry green rubber.
I asked if there was any love.
She replied:
there are few things worse than saying good morning
to someone you said goodbye to, the night before.

Lizard's Wink

Phil isn't like the others.
He wears a suit, or blazer and flannels,
circles the back of my head like a boxer.
On his toes, hands darting with the scissors.
One wall of the barber's shop is lined with red shelves
floor to artexed ceiling, empty.
In a recess next to the first washbasin
hugging the beam of a single spotlight
like a superstar, the green iguana.
Staring back with the stored resentment
of a million years, dry skin twitching,
a hairsbreadth away from being stuffed.
Phil used to work cruise ships
unlike the others he initiates conversation
tells me how he threw up over the woman
he was pushing back to her cabin,
sleeping in her wheelchair.
It was the shudder of the lift that did it,
not the giddy roll of Atlantic swell.
He left her still sleeping, her husband later wondering
how she vomited over the back of her head.
Phil doesn't have his name on the mirror:
I'll be off soon, he says, returning the lizard's wink.

Staff Room

There is coffee but no mug. Teachers sit around.
the atmosphere is one of desolation. I am waiting
to begin a morning of poetry with form II.
This lump of a woman descends on me.
The poet, yes? I concede, for once the title is appropriate.
She had recorded her whole life in a book of poetry
which she lost when she moved from Margate to Merthyr.
But now she's written more - could she send me some?
Of course - I scribble an imaginary address,
Don't take the risk of her not losing that.

Skin

She watches over her book.
Skin tells the story of his day
pinched on the bridge of his nose
the indent of his glasses
just removed,
his arms tied by
veins like the lines of fat round a faggot.
He bends, unbalanced, hops,
pulls off his socks,
rings around his ankles
lines of pressure.
He drops his pants
on his stomach the welt
of his belt.

She closes the book.
He knots the pyjama cord
pain floats from the marrow of his bones
hovers beneath the surface of his skin,
inside his eyeballs, flutters against his inner ear
flowers as easily as pleasure once did.
She folds back the cover
lets her husband in.
Skin, it's all over him.

Stood Up

She stands in shadow
leaning back against the wall
only her feet edge sunlight.
She feels the coolness of stone

through her thin blouse,
remembers the smile on his face
the boy with shining black hair.
Now she knows he was mocking her.

Next year she will break their hearts
these boys with their lying eyes,
stride through their lives on her long legs
trample their desires under her brilliant shoes.

But now she stares out of shadow
the features of her face obliterated
as if wiped out by the stroke
of an artist's brush.

Wedding Day

In the garden a woman bends to her weeding.
She smiles at the garage boys
taking a rest from making their noise
next to a van with the legend *Tool Hire Reading*
Many miles from here her family gathers but
my mother has declined her invitation to the wedding.

> *In the presbytery alone and hunched*
> *as if the space above him were too heavy to bear*
> *a terminally-ill priest polishes*
> *the silver communion goblet with*
> *all the time in the world.*
> *Coolness keeps the scent of flowers.*

She prunes with relish, now it's the clematis.
There are framed photos in the living room
one taken at Aberystwyth on her honeymoon.
It was a hot day such as this.
Is it six years since her husband died?
She thinks again how cruel fate is.

> *Above us eternally bleeding a crucifix towers.*
> *Feet shuffle over freshly lacquered oak,*
> *the church rustles her trousseau of light.*
> *Outside a voice demands the presence*
> *of the bride's mother and her brother.*
> *At the top of the steps we pause.*

She microwaves frozen chips, a slice of pork,
eats Walls Viennetta sitting at the kitchen table
pours tea, addresses Betsi, as if the cat were able
to reply, in Welsh. After her meal she'll go for a walk
perhaps to the end of the street or across the Green
maybe meet a neighbour, for a few minutes talk.

The priest nods, grimaces, grinds his jaws,
what he has to do in God's service!
Why do they always mumble their vows?
Bridesmaids' red hair falls over
crushed blue velvet, burns bare skin:
of this shot, there is a re-take.

Tesco's is a short trip to the end of the street.
Down the aisle she walks, picks up and squints
at a packet of Fox's Glacier Mints.
She chooses a lamb chop from the rows of meat,
at the checkout refuses her change
on the grounds that the note is counterfeit.

Then a dash by taxi to pick up the doomed cake
three tiers in lettuce boxes, broken leaves of icing
collecting like polystyrene packing chips,
empty cake stand a snake about to strike.
Later we eat gobbets of ostrich in a
restaurant partly owned by Bob Geldof.

The lottery prize has doubled.
She checks the numbers of her single entry -
births, deaths, a life's inventory:
the year her sister Mari and Tom got wed.
She never wins but there is sweeter pleasure
as she is alive and they are dead.

John is arseholed, back from Dusseldorf
pogoing with the boys wild-eyed with booze.
The groom's mother watches with her lover.
We stack presents into a supermarket trolley.
We'll never get a taxi, but with the extravagance of drunks
we order three when two would do.

My mother locks her bedroom door.
In the darkness the wireless and its sound of static.
Just another day - no more, no less dramatic.
Tomorrow there'll be a call from her new in-law.
She does not regret missing the wedding;
now obituaries interest her more.

Stealth

They stand around in celebration
country people, smiling, old -
a woman holds a jug of raki
offers drinks to the journalists.

There is only the wing of the stealth bomber,
this undetectable machine of destruction
its $42 million worth of radar - invisible
technology riddled with bullet holes,
stencilled aluminium stuffed with formaldehyde foam
like a gutted fridge on the town dump.

We smile back at the television screen
enjoy their triumph, our fellow Europeans.
In Kosovo, the sons of these Serbs
employ less sophisticated brutality:
rape women, raze homes, herd refugees.

And we say: not here, not us, not now, not ever.
But tonight the after-burners of British jets
will scorch the air over Belgrade.
A jug of raki will rattle on the sideboard,
and we are all diminished.

Assembly Lines

There's a pornographic movie playing in my head
Tony Blair and Wales are getting into bed.

Alun Michael's dropped in just to say hello.
Hold her down says Tony while I give her my manifesto.
Rhodri's locked in the attic and Ron has gone walkabout:
the cameras are rolling and Alun's all smiles -
it's the age old story - before the rogering, the lies.

Rod Richard's in the corner playing with himself
now Wales is the best thing since sliced bread.
Like Thatcher, Rod wants to stuff the Welsh
He's a pimp - don't believe a word he's said.

Wigley's pontificating saying this is not very nice
then he adds *Twll din pob Sais.*

And the Lib Dems hang around like groupies at a show
hoping when Labour's finished Alun will give them a go.

It's a sorry spectacle which doesn't fill you with hope
perhaps they'll hang themselves, given so much rope.

We need to employ more guile:
Let poets write the policies
Let sculptors shape our world
Let artists paint the future.
This way Wales will win
or at least we'll fail in style.

Dance This Way

He's a sort of style survivor,
Tee shirt baggy trousers,
could be an artist, not poor, not rich,
not quite at the last ditch.

She's definitely of now:
post-post-feminist, bodywise, knows it.
Moves like her limbs
are on ball bearings

He's old enough to feel regret.
She's young enough to make him sweat.

'Move like me' she shouts
as strobe lights chase her
all over the floor -
but his head is down, his arms are pumping,

I've danced this way for 30 years
I'll dance this way until time disappears.

I
    Danced this way to Mayall's blues
    Danced this way in platform shoes
    Danced this way all though my teens
    Danced this way in torn blue jeans
    Danced this way in a silk kaftan
    Danced this way after Vietnam
    Danced this way to spitting punk
    Danced this way to disco funk
    Danced this way on the Isle of Wight
    And
    I'll dance this way tonight.

Swansea Station

That man's so drunk
he's missed his train
corners a woman
demands to be kissed
again and again.
His face looks like a painting
when she knees him in the bollocks
not a Constable
more like one of Jackson Pollock's.

Ritual

The sea's the colour of cooked liver.
He stands on stones, water to his chin
arms flapping aimlessly.
She watches from the shore
sitting on his coat
knees pulled to her chest.

This is the birthday ritual.
What used to be a brisk swim
through crashing surf
is now an immersion in the
slop of South Wales industrial waste.

She remembers how he used to run
out of the waves like a lifeguard.
Today it's a trek from the water's edge.
She tosses him a towel: *Good?*
Great, so invigorating. His flesh
is as lumpy as the Bristol Channel.

She smiles, braces herself.
There's more of this to come.

Looser

He's a tough bastard,
a wild fucker, I wouldn't like to cross.
OK when he's sober, after drink unstable
as old gelignite and just as sweaty.
He's always there in the entrance to the pub
his glass in his hand or on that single table
between the bog door and the stairs.
That night he clocked me coming in
as if he owned the place.
Eyes as sharp as a shit house rat
new tattoos on his arms
he slides me an *alright?*
out of the corner of his mouth.
I nod, keep moving.
When I leave it's late, I see him in the lane
legs braced against the alcohol,
his finger moving between two guys
like the needle of a cheap compass.
His lips are looser now. He says:
It's not business like - where's the professionalism?
Broken glass reflects the street light
as tangible as their fear.
There's a look on his face that says
someone's going to pay.

Telephone

In work a secretary answers my phone
checks with me whether I want the call
and then puts it through.
At home I answer the phone.
It's always for my daughter.
I have to check with her
whether she wants the call
then I put it through.

Minibar

A rare night in a plush hotel
sleepless under a sleek duvet
drone of arterial traffic
slipping time zones, a dateline crossed
yesterday, or was it tomorrow?

Thick carpet caresses
gullible bare feet round the bed
guided by the light of the minibar.
Its mock regency door thrown open
a wrecker's beacon to wavering resolve
rewards my gaze with a gurgle of refrigerant.
Somewhere behind the Toblerone
a motor gently boils.

I was seduced by the
silent steel lift
plastic entry card
73 channel TV
bathroom goodies
the prairie of chintz
but the hum of the minibar
whispers like the forbidden sea
in the shell of my memory.

Teeny bottles of exotic booze
pistachio in jars
Kalamata olives like grapes
Droste almond pastilles
Bahlsen chocolate wafers
Crunch cream ginger wafers
Macadamia pecans and praline puffs
Becks beer and Dom Perignon.

In the mercury light
of midnight TV
tin sliced ring pulls
rattled gold wrappings
savaged plastic packaging
destroyed bottles
litter my hotel dream.

Next morning I sign the debt warrant
mouth as dry as credit slip counterfoils.

Garnish

Why, why? he blubbers
fighting back tears.
He whoops a cough/sneeze
unwittingly lets the bogey go.
His palm covers his nose too late,
he watches its descent across
the hostile space between them.
It lands on her last meatball
balanced on a tiny nose hair
touching yet not touching
undetected.

Her neck goes red when she's upset
now it's as hot as radioactivity
because, because... she struggles to explain
because it's over, yes over...
but you promised forever..
you were different then, you've changed.
Hasn't he heard this somewhere before?

Her fork ventures near the meatball.
How can she tell him there is someone else?
His pathos makes her angry, hungry.
She offers: *I did love you - so much.*
In a way some part of you will always be inside me.
She spears the meat ball.
Her jaws snap like a predatory fish.

He is silent as she chews.
He watches something move
in the glowing sleeve of her throat.
Already he feels much better.

The Colour of Sex

On the beach, tits are everywhere.
Comes as a shock to a North European male -
all sizes from massive moored dirigibles
to the slightest undulation, the wink of a nipple.
Then there's the suntanned skin
female legs kicking gloriously through surf
bikini bottoms as big as big toe nail varnish
pubic hairs scribbling the edge.

But there's no sex.
The sex has been bleached out.

The colour of sex is in the
froth of underwear, of stretched
fabric wanting to be undone
eyelid flickers
zips, clasps
clothes
kicked to the floor
the shadow of a spider
scuttling under the bedroom door.

Artist - for Frank Auerbach

It begins with a lump in my mind.
Tyrannical youth kneeling in a bog of paint.
Stella's pale body the wreck of constraint.
In Australia they hung him upside down.

In the threatening flux of experience
he feels the need for stability.
Painting is not a mysterious activity.
Old newspapers hang on the line

For two years and three hundred sittings
back and forth his gaze beating
against the unseeable, the unmakeable
scrubbed back to a grey blur

the ghost of erased images.
A painting is the sum of its destructions.
Hidden encoded instructions.
Archaic stoniness, studied inelegance.

Pure and buttery in their tins
ochre, green and cadmium red
set fire to the *Nude on Bed*.
A bright epiphany of raw materials.

The head of Michael Podro
weeps in the gloom.
So much paint it creeps around the room
and Mrs Lessore's shoes watch you go.

First Love

My first long term relationship
was with a red handkerchief
Uncle Jack gave me
not for my birthday, but on his.

A coal man who needed to mop his brow frequently
he had a large supply, so when he ripped open the flat box
It was to me he handed the crisp square of linen.
That first night I took it to bed.

After some quick preliminaries
(I was inexperienced then, knowing little of foreplay)
I had my way with the red hanky.
The next morning it had a different sort of crispness.

I stashed it under the mattress
kept it like a mistress
used it to satisfy my
post-pubescent lust, fuelled by creased

glossy, black and white photographs
which circulated the playground
shown to me by sniggering boys
at least two forms higher.

Women with nice smiles
big breasts and airbrushed pudenda
more often than not in outdoor locations.
My mother never told me when she found it.

I was walking home and saw the red handkerchief
up there on the clothes line with the sheets,
flying like a warning against dangerous tides.
Uncle Jack's hanky arrived back

Neatly folded in the drawer
next to my underwear
condemned by maternal approval
and an overdose of Robin starch.

I left it in its ironed aloofness
preferring the less erotic allure
of one night stands with
extracted exercise book pages.

Clock

Next I drink in the Albert.
No one speaks. I lean on the bar.
There's a railway clock.
Men alone, standing, sitting,
fixed and strategic as pieces in
a forgotten chess game.
In the corner the only woman
sits with a fat man staring
at the blank television.
It's as quiet as a reference library.
A priest arrives with a suitcase
walks up to the fat man.
They exchange a few words
then they leave. The woman
picks over an empty packet of peanuts.

From here on in

I bought a black tie especially for Glyn's funeral
reckoned I'd be needing my own from here on in.
We got to the crem early and I walked
around the grounds, found my father's
commemorative kerbstone: no date,
just his name HOPKIN IVOR THOMAS.
A jay flew across the garden
flaunting its inappropriate plumage.

My mother had fallen into conversation
with a woman who had arrived early.
Everybody comes too early to the crem.
The last time she had been here
one of the mourners had died during the service.

My mother enjoyed the funeral.
Neither of Glyn's wives turned up
but his two children huddled
with their grandmother on the front pew,
appropriately grief-stricken.

She left her black jacket in my car.
I hung it in the wardrobe next
to my father's unwearably huge overcoat.
Later she told me she'd bought a pink jacket:
*The next funeral I go to will be my own
and I would like to wear this new jacket.*
I said I'd arrange it. Put the phone down,
thought of my mother awaiting the furnace.
Some competition for the jay.

The Interview

The next candidate sits down.
He's a cocky bastard.
The wall is breaking, the muscles in my back are becoming disconnected,
slipping their anchorage points.
A month ago I knelt for the milk bottle,
could hear the tissues tearing, ligaments snapping.

I look the candidate in the eye,
lenses still elastic engage my presbyopic vision.
I take revenge on his youth,
relish his nervousness, ask him questions
that cause the sweat to bead on his public school lip.
If only he knew what was in the bag
in my office, the new office overlooking the bay:
vaginal lubricant, Johnson baby lotion,
large pack of rubbers, Kleenex man-size tissues, hemorrhoid
cream.
I shift position, the vertebrae don't fit any more.
They grind the discs. I tried traction.
It doesn't work. I went to an osteopath
who did Groucho Marx impersonations.

Tonight more of my middle aged love affair
and the horror of sex - full frontal sex.
Will it be her or me that turns the light out first?
Perhaps I should remove the light bulb just in case.
She's so dry: is that because she finds me unattractive?
I ask the candidate -*does the juice flow out of your women?*

Trapezius, deltoid, latissimus dorsi,
my back muscles squabble like children
then retreat from each other in a hot sulk.
He is unzipping his portfolio. I ask to see
his diploma project and his prostate gland.

The project is uninspiring but the gland
is good. I take out mine and compare.
His of course is pink and resilient and flexible.
Mine is bigger but hard and fibrous
like a winter radish that's been left
too long in the ground.

What's more she'll want to be adventurous,
nothing worse than a middle-aged woman
rediscovering sex from the wreckage of a lost marriage,
the years of just going through the motions,
the years of not even going through the motions.
God save me from the blow jobs, the improvisations,
the shy gestures to sadism.
Last week my cock was rubber,
I squeezed the blood to the end, fed it into her
a lame ferret set to fetch a long gone rabbit.

I ask the candidate
what will you bring to the job?
Vaginal lubricant, Johnson baby lotion,
large pack of rubbers, Kleenex man-size tissues
hemorrhoid cream.
Will you take her gluteus maximus in your hands?
Will you slip into my bed, fuck her for me
so that in the morning she'll say
Wow you were good last night,
you were something else, I could
feel you pumping, you filled me
up like a car at a petrol station.
Will you lend me a few lost vertebrae
so that I can get my back back?

The candidate gathers his things, was not successful.
He did not have the required qualities for the job.

Uncle Dewi's Lump

Uncle Dewi was tough, ex-copper
won medals in the war killing Italians.
More than once he wiped
a dead man's breakfast from his bayonet.

Dewi nearly blew himself up
when he tossed a grenade back.
Got showered by bits of enemy
and had a lump on his head ever since.

Until one summer that is,
when we were on the train
going to Tenby. His head ached
and he was grumpy as hell.

Doris had a look,
pulled off the lump with her fingers.
Turned out to be the Italian's tooth.
Been carrying it around for twenty years.

Can I keep it? I asked.
"What for you daft bugger?"
He tossed the last mortal remains
of the Italian out of the train.

Pity, said Doris:
it was the only real tooth
he had in his head.

The Eagle of the Heart

He wanted sons, the Cardiff-Italian,
to kick a ball with, to join him under the bonnet of his car,
to share a lager when boxing was on the telly.
Instead he got daughters, stunning fizzing
redheads who at the age of fifteen
were known as the twins from hell.

They battered each other rolling in the street,
got sent home from school for knocking out
two teeth of the prefect who reprimanded them
for dismantling the wall bars in the gym.
They took it in turns to run away from home
and then, what's worse, to return.

He's developed this knack
of knowing that the knock on the door
is another aggrieved parent, teacher, neighbour.
Or now, more frequently, a policeman
who naively thinks that a stern ticking off
from an officer of the law, will make
some sort of difference to the girls who stand
angelically in front of him, their heads bowed,
their faces grimacing from the pain of *not* laughing out loud.

At times like these, he goes to his garage,
peers alone at the grisly innards of his old BMW
as if somehow the future is written there
in oil, in damaged wires, in the white fur
growing on the scabious black skin
of the Exide heavy-duty battery.

Doors

How can I forget these doors made of mahogany
on trestles, and me, the apprentice, sanding
every square inch? Gideon Delahay, craftsman,
joiner, with his kettle of warm water, approaches
through the rushing noise of the machine shop.
Mahogany is deceitful, the grain can run both ways.
He doesn't say much, Delahay, watches with
those narrow eyes, his face cut in half by
the shadow of the pulled peak of his flat cap.
As he tips the kettle, drops of water fall from
the burnt metal, catch the light, mercury in the dust.
Water raises the texture of this wood like
a hand running up the fur of a cat's back.
I pick up my sanding block, get to work
this time coming from the other direction.

Drag and push, drag and push
I hear this noise in the night
as my father sucks mustard gas in the trench
of his dreams. Sweat tracks my labourer's makeup
and hardwood dust burns my lungs.
This is the last job I will do on the tools.
I watch Gideon Delahay hang the doors
in the façade of the Bute Street bank,
close them easy as if they ran on ball bearings.

I walked through them only yesterday.
There was a twinge of kinetic memory in
my biceps as I touched the iron surface.
It was that or arthritis. One world war,
two marriages, a heart attack, eighty years.
Pain visits the darkness of my body like meteors.

They are standing straighter than me, these doors.

Love spoons

Standing alone in the love spoon shop
I couldn't help but be envious of them.
Man all smiles,
woman tossing the wind from her hair,
beautiful, so much in love.
But something happened while I read about the spoons,
entwined hearts,
symbols of everlasting happiness and joy.

They were standing at the counter
her face flushed with anger.
He must have touched a raw nerve
opened an old wound:
If you don't shut up I'll stick
this spoon right up your arse...
Her lips were tight and bloodless:
And yes...,
she composed herself for the shop assistant,
we'll take the big one.

I want to be one of Neil's girlfriends

I want to be one of Neil's girlfriends
I hope he can squeeze me in
After girlfriend
Number 1,2,3,4…
After all, there are seven days in the week.
Neil is my ideal man
Neil epitomizes the grand plan
Neil hasn't got any diseases
Neil does as he pleases
Neil is complete in every detail
I'll return to being foetal
If Neil doesn't let me be
One of his girlfriends.
Neil is quieter than a vacuum cleaner
Neil is cleverer than a big dick
Neil has more clout than my hammer
Neil has better knees than a queen bee
Neil is not a chauvinist
He told me so.
If Neil fell out of a plane
He'd walk on the air
If Neil were an academic he'd hold a chair
If Neil were a writer
He'd win the Nobel Prize
If Neil were a burglar
He'd be a master of disguise.
I know Neil doesn't say I love you
Unless it's to get a screw
But I'm mad about Neil
I can't help the way I feel
Neil is a fucking machine
Neil is a dream
The way I feel about Neil is obscene
I want him so much
IT MAKES ME SCREAM

I'll leave my semi detached
Throw up my family and friends
Turn my back on the patio
Leave the Mondeo in the drive
Without Neil I won't be able to survive.
But, I hear you say,
You're a man and Neil's not gay
I don't give a damn
I'll have a sex change operation
I'll even change the wallpaper
In my bedroom
Just to be
One of Neil's girlfriends.

I'm smoking with Lolita

I'm smoking with Lolita
I'm smoking with Lolita
I'm sitting, smoking
Joking with Lolita
Lolita, Lolita
THERE'S NO GIRL WHO IS SWEETER
I'm smoking with Lolita
I'm joking with Lolita
Lolita comes from Brazil
Lolita speaks Portuguese
Lolita makes me go weak at the knees
Lolita said please
Have you a light?
I'm smoking with Lolita
I'm drinking with Lolita
Lolita, Lolita
I WISH THAT YOU COULD MEET HER
Lolita, Lolita

I'm living with Lolita
Living with Lolita
We are talking
She is smiling
I'm moving with Lolita
I'm flying with Lolita
She is with me in São Paulo
I can feel the heat
Of the South American sun
I'm smoking with Lolita
I'm burning with Lolita
Rub that oil on me Lolita
Make me sticky Lolita
I am happy with Lolita
PERHAPS ONE DAY YOU'LL MEET HER
I'm smoking with Lolita

I'm sleeping with Lolita
I'm dreaming with Lolita
I'm dreaming, I'm smoking
I'm dreaming
I'm dreaming
I'm dreaming

Awake but sleepy
My memory's getting weaker
Put more coins in the meter
I wish I were
Still smoking with Lolita   Lolita   Lolita.

Anywhere but somewhere else

The poet sits alone in the front pew
behind him empty too
but the rest of the church is packed.
People stand at the back.
Why does the poet sit alone?
The poet sits alone because here
he represents the devil.
The dead man is
an atheist and therefore now in hell.
The dead man's coffin,
blistered by a shower of rain
is parked in the aisle.
After the lesson, John Chapter 11
verses 21 to 27,
the clergy nods to the poet.
It's time for the dead man's favourite poem,
from one manic depressive to another

> *Oh to break loose like a Chinook salmon*
> *jumping and falling back*
> *nosing up to the impossible*
> *stone the bone crushing water fall*
> *raw jawed weak fleshed there*
> *stopped by ten steps of the roaring ladder and then*
> *to clear the top at the last try*
> *alive enough to spawn and die.*

So far so good. The canon's flesh
creeps into the folds of his cassock.
The poet knows the lines.
He is reading the faces of the congregation.
Their stares fix him like nails
blank as the holes of woodworm in the church roof.
Gradually the silent horrible dawning-
this poem is about hypocrisy

this poem is blasphemy.

> *Oh bible chopped and crucified*
> *In hymns we hear but do not read*
> *They sing of peace and preach despair.*

The canon goes off inaudibly.
Old ladies explode silently.
Church elders shift uncomfortably without even moving;
faces scream silently violently disapproving,
sympathisers applaud in their heads.
There is a silent cacophony
of protest, confusion and joy.

The poem ends.
The poet, bent double against the silence
resumes his seat.
The canon has been struck dumb.
Time stops.
The church has entered another dimension.
It is a space ship exploring a black hole of silence.
And then the coffin creaks
as the deceased speaks:
Goodbye friends I loved you all
or at least most of you
or perhaps some part of all of you:
forgive my poet friend
poets so rarely come to a good end.

Reassured by the dead man
the congregation rises to its feet.
The canon motions to the pall bearers.
The coffin is carried out.
Later at the crem
the poet lights a cigarette
blinks back a tear as the smoke blows in his eyes.

Last chance of understanding

I could never imagine you
my father in a wheelchair.
It arrived too late
folded and wrapped in polythene.
I shifted the bulky package around the house
eventually to the garage.
Even the hospital was slow to reclaim it
unpacked unused
the last few years of your life.

You too were moved around the house
and then you never left the bedroom.
Why was it so hard for me
the special effort
to walk up the stairs
to stay and talk?

Lifting you out of the bed
I was often too rough
bruising the skin under your arms
skin that was as
soft as oil on water.
I balanced you on the toilet
me impatient, wishing you would hurry up
wishing sometimes
you'd hurry up and die.

The doctor called an ambulance
his lips close to the receiver
as he arranged a ward
suitable for a terminal case.
Upstairs
my mother emptied the urine bag
for the last time.

Strange confessional, the single bed ward
hidden as you were behind the grille of pain.
Did you hear me?
The gap of thirty years of different lives
you always so sure, so straight;
me never knowing what I wanted.
But it was too late
to build a bridge into your world
bounded by the bars of a hospital bed.

I held your hand
fingers stiff as wire
as you in delirium spoke to your father.
And although you spoke in Welsh
I guessed that you too
were trying to take
a last chance of understanding,
son to father son to father
unheard monologues over generations.

The anxieties of life
overtook the anguish of inevitable death.
We were afraid no one would come to the funeral
you being so close and private.
The undertaker said there was nothing worse
than fine Welsh hymns
and a lone voice to sing them.
But the chapel was packed.
Yours was a memory worth honouring.

As we drove home
I thought of your father
whom I never knew
and you
whose hand I never held
until the fingers
were frozen with pain.

Butlins chalet rap

6 pints of lager
3 brandy shandies
1 don't sneak up behind me and
A long screw against the wall.
Which ever is nearest love
You can call me anything you like
Except early in the morning
Yes 4x will do
Just give me the Australian
Are you pregnant?
No? well you bloody well should be
Can't you take a joke?
Can't you take an overdose?
Single parents come and meet
For an icebreaker in the touchdown club.
Dame Edna is the winner
Frankenstein is highly commended.
Men - keep fit with Fiona
The Autumn club always meets in the Mayfair Suite
OK forget the long screw against the wall
Give me another don't sneak up on me.
Do you want a tray?
I'd prefer it in a glass.
Glamorous Granny my arse
I've seen more meat on a butcher's biro.
After the family knockout
The half boarders will play the self caterers
At football
And we still need jockeys
For the donkey derby.
There were traffic jams on the Severn Bridge
You shouldn't have come through Clifton
Please give your names to Redcoat Dave.

Conversations with a stoned dog

It was the day that the dog
ate my last big piece of dope
I almost gave up hope
I was full of despair
one minute it was sitting there
on the kitchen chair
the next gone
the dog just looking at me
a smile on his face.

I chased him round and round the flat
until I managed to lay him out
on the kitchen mat
forced salty water down his throat
trying to get him to puke
but the dog said
Hey man - I know this stuff makes you
thirsty but I'd prefer a lager.

So I took the dog out to get some air
me thinking this just isn't fair -
you getting stoned on my dope
and Jack - he's a Russell
is saying love and peace brother
to all the cats in town
and I'm thinking- can a dog OD?

After that I took him home
tried to tempt him with a bone
but that dog just wanted
to sit around philosophizing
talking about sex
and a certain Afghan hound that had taken his fancy.
That bitch has a great arse
he growled confidentially.

I said that he had a lot of nerve
for a Russell
it's a well known fact that Afghans go for dogs
with a lot of muscle
like Dobermans and Rottweilers.
Jack said 'what about passion?'
the dog was getting misty eyed.
That's out of fashion
it's all carnal now, I replied.

Jack was sad
he'd been in love with the Afghan for years
totally ignored
he needed to make a gesture of love
like Van Gogh
I know he said
I'll get my balls cut off.

Personally I thought this drastic
but mindful of the cash
I offered to do it with a piece of elastic.
Jack said no:
I need the surgeon's knife
To give my life a new direction
Forget the bitch. I don't want to be a man
If I can't have the Afghan.

Well the next day
we went and had him done.
He wasn't quite so philosophical
when the anaesthetic had worn off
but then life has its compensations
now he sees the Afghan every day:
castrated, she prefers him that way.
He doesn't pose a threat.
They are great pals - oh and good news

I found the stuff
hidden in a neat pile
of vomit under the bed.
Now Jack and I often share a pipe
that and a can of Red Stripe
not salty water.
In my conversations with the stoned dog
he tries to persuade me
to get my balls cut off:
women will find you irresistible
and he makes a sort of purring noise.

Despite everything
I still think of Jack as one of the boys.

Going to see Lou Reed

She said
I'm going to see Lou Reed.
I said really, where?
She said here, in town.
I said is he still alive?
Walking on the wild side
with Warhol, Nico, Cale
and those.
Did any of them survive the 'sixties?
If they did, they shouldn't have.
People don't know when to stop
when to call it a day
when it's out of time
all blown out
finished
run dry
finis
kaput.

Still for old time's sake
I'll come.
She said
You'll be there anyway.
I said I will?
She said
I said I was going to see you read.
I said me? Read with Lou Reed?
She said forget it.
I think I'll stay at home
and listen to a record.

False teeth

The pub is like the poetry group
a grand venture in decline.
Five people sitting at a table:
it is nearly stop tap and typically
two have only just arrived.
One has been there for hours
making desultory conversation
with the old man
whose elaborate NHS walking stick
leans against the table.
The woman in the group
is uneasy, thinking
probably correctly
that the magazine she is editing
will never appear.
The other initiates conversation
which ranges from Madonna's clothes
to book cover designs.
Three of the group attempt to decipher
the writing of one
who is present
but cannot remember what
he was writing about.
There is silence.
Private thoughts turn to the
possibility of attending car maintenance
classes instead of struggling along
with poets.
There is a clatter.
All five turn.
The man with the many legged
walking stick has sneezed.
His false teeth have flown
out of his mouth
and now sit on the floor

smiling up at the writers.
Unperturbed
he reaches out with his stick
drags back the teeth
dusts them off and
returns them to his mouth.
Behind the bar the American barmaid
has discovered that Budweisers
are not the same as Barbicans.
Her face dissolves into gloom
as we listen to singing from the other bar -
a man who thinks he's sober will later climb into his car
drive home without a care in the world.

Conditioning Room

Rectangular weights
threaded on stainless steel
seats
straps
pulleys
bars
things that can be adjusted
tables that can be turned
or tilted
mirrors
extract fans
and men sweating
SM freaks in the conditioning room.

Fetishists
with head bands
sweat bands
track suit bottoms
towels
enjoying the Saturday morning wank
you ejaculate through your pores.

You walk in
choose a machine
one which is free
perhaps still wet with the sweat
of your predecessor
feel the steel
grip the plastic handles
and go at it
grunt groan
grunt groan.
Give it all you've got
embrace the machine
grunt groan gasp collapse

rest.
The machine is ideal
passive pliable
you use it as you please
ride the rowing machine
snatch the oars
make the hydraulics hiss
feel the seat slide easy under your buttocks
then hear the machine scream
GIVE IT ONE FOR THE LONG BORING HOURS IN THE OFFICE
GIVE IT ONE FOR THE PRICK WHO PUT YOU DOWN
GIVE IT ONE FOR THE GIRL YOU DID NOT MAKE.
Stop.

Try another machine.
You can use them all
insert your steel peg
choose your weight
make it easy
make it hard.
There's nothing to worry about
you won't catch a disease
you can walk away
just pull out your peg
pick up your towel
leave your sweat on the floor.

Next time
pause at the door
see the men
pouring their furious impotent energy
into the receptive machines
and
understand the mechanics of the conditioning room.

Migration

Sandwich in plastic birth sac
Cling film:
Plasticized, polyvinyl chloride to which has been added dioctyl
adipate and dioctyl phathalate. These chemicals give pvc its
qualities of cling and stretch and constitute 40% of the film.

Discarded it shrivels.
He bites.

The plasticizers leach into the food due to their high solubility in
lipids.

Mouth works
soft clean blown steamed wwwwwwwhite.

When plasticized pvc film is wrapped around fatty foods the
dioctyl adipate and dioctyl phathalate leach into the food. This
process is known as migration.

Polyunsaturated
processed, tasting of
stainless steel
Kraft cheese like fresh putty.

To achieve the required levels of gloss, clarity, cling stretch
To achieve the required levels of gloss, clarity, cling stretch
To achieve the required levels of gloss, clarity, cling stretch
British manufacturers have increased the levels of dioctyl
adipate and dioctyl phathalate. Tests weighing film before and
after immersion in olive oil (an approved lipid substitute) have
shown that up to 25% of the film can migrate into the food
which it is supposed to protect.

He wipes his lips
swallows the last soft morsel
notices the translucence of his skin.
Later he ties his shoelaces
without bending over.

This process is known as migration

Bogwiser

Men understand about household chores.
They know that the shopping has to be done
now and then
food has to be cooked
sometimes
dishes have to be washed and put away
if there's time
the carpet has to be hoovered
once in a blue moon.
BUT LAVATORIES
BUT LAVATORIES - LAVATORIES ALWAYS CLEAN
THEMSELVES.
It's one of the miracles of life
I suppose
that lavatories always clean themselves -
no matter how vomit stained
or shit blitzed
that bog will be clean again
tomorrow.

When she went
I realised that a clean bog
has something to do with women.

I've thought about this and now I've realised
that the bog does it.
It wants to impress
so it cleans itself like a bird.
Now she's gone
it sees no need.
The sparkle has deserted its porcelain
and it has let itself go terribly
worse than me.
I've tried shouting at it:
pull yourself together pan

cajoling
whispered sweet nothings into the cistern,
said *come on Armitage, she'll be back soon*.
But that bog isn't stupid
it will not be deceived.
Wallowing in self pity
I've given up with it
and taken to crapping elsewhere.

My sister's back from college

My sister's back from college
and there are strange tubs in the fridge
which I must not touch
because only students
eat yoghurt.

She had a trunk bought her to go away
and was very brave
when the train pulled out
hardly managing a wave
to me
a mere schoolboy.

She's got a green scarf
with white stripes
which I must not wear
because it's a college scarf
and in Swansea
she lives in a flat.

Her best friend is a Greek
who's got a boyfriend
who drinks a bottle of Ouzo a day.
I'm impressed
more than I care to say.

And there are books in her bedroom
some with hard covers
and long titles
which she does not read
and paperbacks
she hides from my mother
which I read.

But in 1969 I had my time

rolling marbles under police horse hooves
in Grosvenor Square
and smoking
which did not impress my mate
who was a roadie with Ten Years After
and had a way with women
although not my sister
who was a youth employment officer
and lived in Rugby.

Empty House

He pressed his blade into the wood
feeling the steel slide
and then withdrawing it slowly.

He jumped up and down on the wooden floors.
He shut doors
and ran his finger around the gap.

He opened the trap to the attic
and there in the light of his torch
rubbed his fingers on the chimney breast.

Standing outside in the garden
he counted loose slates
stared long and hard at the face of the house.

Down in the basement he felt a draught on his skin.
He pressed his hands on the decaying surface,
peered hard into each dark recess.

His knuckles rapped the plaster
of the walls in the hall.
His eyes checked off cracks in the cornice.

Making only a few notes in his stiff covered book
he emerged from the house
shut the door firmly and slipped the key through the letter
box.

The first thing he would do when he returned
would be to wash his hands
before writing the report.

Later, in the overheated office, a typist
would type on one side of paper
what one hundred years mean to a house.

Sliced Life

He wrapped his life in cling film
and put it in the fridge of his marriage.

He made love only on Fridays and Saturdays
because the sheets were changed
on Sundays.
He drank moderately
occasionally.

He worked diligently
and was kind to his wife.

When he died he dreamed he was
a slice of salami
which had slowly curled up at the edges.

He saw the salami
reflected in the undertaker's eyes
as he was measured for the coffin
which appeared later.
But he was rescued by his wife and put between two slices of
bread
to make
a salami sandwich.

Lying on the kitchen table
he saw his wife
clear out the fridge.
Although she was too old to take a lover
she ate out
and frequently went
to the pictures.

Touch

The two women
rode home alone in the van.
One was pregnant
with a husband and lover.
Her friend said
you are beautiful
and what a fine bulge -
let me feel your bump
let me touch your unborn child.
The pregnant woman blushed
when she saw her friend's eyes shining.
She remembered the way
her men turned away from her.
Together they climbed into the back
and she undid her maternity trousers.
Her friend's smooth hand slid over her stomach,
up and down
over and round
smoothing
her stretched skin.
She closed her eyes:
that woman's hand should shape the world.
They drove home
and kissed gently on the cheek
when they parted.

I think of Julie Walters

I think of Julie Walters
when I scratch my ears.
I KNEW HER WHEN SHE WAS A NURSE
not a star.

She told me:
in work I slip off to the lavatory
with a cotton bud
IT'S BLISS
better than a fag.

Once through half-open eyes
I saw her turn her head
to throw back her long hair
and insert the blue stick
like a hypodermic
into her ear.
Her face froze with pleasure
as her fingers turned
SEARCHING
for the right spot.

Later
when she was drunk
she said
IF YOU GO TOO FAR
YOU CAN'T COME BACK
BUT LIFE'S LIKE THAT.

Now I imagine her
alone in her dressing room
the door closed
on the adoring applause

her fingers
spinning
a thin stick of
cotton wool.

Digging deep in the freezer

They said *dig deep*.
So I did
deep into my chest freezer.
I found him
halfway down
and pulled him out.

I cut the policeman's head off,
I did it with a chain saw.
He'd been in the freezer for a week
so he didn't bleed
over the garage floor.
The blade did cause a smattering of mince meat
because it got hot I supposed.
Before putting the head back into the freezer
I held it level with mine.
Stubble was pushing through the purple bruises
where he'd banged his face
against the freezer lid
in his desperation to get out.
I noticed a fine hoar frost
over his eyebrows and lashes.
I tapped his eyeball with a screwdriver
it was hard like a glass marble
pale blue like ice
surprised frozen eyes.
I always freeze policemen alive.
I then cut his body into neat pieces
which I wrapped in cling film
before putting it back into the freezer.

The next day they came for him
as I'd arranged.
I always gave them something.
Usually they said:

meat again! thank you very much,
and I would reply:
there's plenty more where that came from.
They would say thank you again.
I will miss the people who collected food for the striking
miners.
They were ever so polite.

I told her I loved her a lot in Splott

I said I'd be sad if
she didn't come to Cardiff.

I called her a sensation
when I met her at Central Station.

I sang like a lark
when we walked in Roath Park.

I said I'd never met any one finer
in Rhiwbina.

I vowed I'd be her man
in Pen-y-lan.

I fell at her feet
in Oakfield Street.

I told her I loved her a lot
in Splott.

I said I liked having you
in Western Avenue.

But our love turned sour
over beer in the Glendower.

She called me a fool
in the Empire Pool.

She broke down and cried
in Riverside,

after I'd let her down
in Grangetown.

She shouted *YOU BRUTE*
in Bute.

So we called it a day
in Manor Way,

the next time, she said,
I'll get an A to Z.

I like my cling film tight

I handed her the sandwich.
She looked disappointed.
I couldn't understand it.
It was her favourite
tomato sauce and spam.

SHE SAID
I like my cling film tight
smooth taut
I want to see my meat neat
pressed tight against the plastic film
a hungry face at the window.

She said I like my cling film tight
smooth taut
ice over the tupperware
a drumskin for impatient fingers
a tense film of anticipation.
She said
I like my cling film taut
smooth taut
if I had my way
I'd wrap the world in cling film
to keep it clean
and free from pollution.

I said *I only offered you a sandwich.*

And once
when I donned this condom
as a prelude to an amorous moment
her eyes lit up.
She said
I LIKE MY CLING FILM TAUT
SMOOTH TAUT

I WANT TO SEE MY MEAT NEAT
PRESSED TIGHT AGAINST THE PLASTIC FILM
A HUNGRY FACE AT THE WINDOW.

But I couldn't stand the tension.

Trip to another planet

The old poet performed well
he was in his element
he knew what he was doing
he fed on the stares of the audience
he affected indifference
to the adoring appreciation
of the well dressed middle aged woman
who hung on to every word, her mouth half open
her lipstick slightly too red.
Even his poem in praise of feminists
was really in praise of his ability
to attract young women.

The poems on this occasion
were not as good as he looked
nicotine stained untidy moustache.
He stabbed the air with his cigarette
and held the plastic beaker of cheap wine
with the reverence normally reserved
for cut glass crystal.

Later in the pub he said
it's all shit out there...
slopping his beer in the general direction
of all establishment figures
who lurk secure behind their double glazing
while he cast himself
as the nagging conscience
of the whole doomed world.

With well practised venom
he spurned the criticisms of an unknown detractor.
If the pub had been less busy
and he'd been assured of an audience
his performance would have continued

with more devastating effect
and sharper material.

As it was
the old poet stood like a colossus
at that point on the literary map
where cheap red wine meets strong Welsh beer
his eyes occasionally cast heavenward
as if preparing
for a trip to another planet.

I think she thinks I think

I think she is counting
the hairs sticking out of my nostrils.

I think she's noticed
my ribcage is distorted and my insteps are disproportionately
high.

I think she's smelling
my sweaty armpits.

I think she's touching my hair
because she can't believe it's so greasy.

I think she thinks I think she's dissatisfied
because I came and she didn't.

I think she's fingering that strange lump under my scrotum
and wondering what it is.

I think she's contemptuous
of my insecurity and inflexibility and the fact that
I need at least two hours sleep a night.

I think she's going to drop me like a brick
when she sees through me.

I think she's not thinking
about me at all.

She says
DON'T THINK
FEEL

I feel
I've got to think things through.